# Acclaim for *1 HOUR PHOTO*

"Phenomenal."
—Colin Thomas, *colinthomas.ca*

"A universal story."
—John Jane, *Review Vancouver*

"A buffet of sensory textures."
—Kathleen Oliver, *Georgia Straight*

"Tetsuro shows himself to be a world-class lateral thinker, master of startling transitions. He can turn on a dime from intimate detail and wry self-mockery to cosmic musings..."
—Lincoln Kaye, *Vancouver Observer*

WINNER OF THE JESSIE RICHARD THEATRE AWARD FOR SIGNIFICANT ARTISTIC ACHIEVEMENT – SMALL THEATRE

Tetsuro Shigematsu, Jamie Nesbitt, and Susan Miyagishima – *1 Hour Photo* – Vancouver Asian Canadian Theatre – Outstanding technical design and execution for the purpose of historical storytelling

T0160396

Also by Tetsuro Shigematsu

# EMPIRE OF THE SON

Published by Talonbooks

# 1 HOUR PHOTO

# 1 HOUR PHOTO

## TETSURO SHIGEMATSU

Foreword by the family of Midge and Karl Ayukawa
Introduction by Naomi Yamamoto
Afterword by Joy Kogawa

Talonbooks

Talonbooks
278 East First Avenue, Vancouver, British Columbia, Canada V5T 1A6
talonbooks.com

Talonbooks is located on xʷməθkʷəy̓əm, Sḵwx̱wú7mesh, and səl̓ilwətaʔɬ Lands.

First printing: 2018

Typeset in Arno
Printed and bound in Canada on 100 percent post-consumer recycled paper

Cover design by Tetsuro Shigematsu, photography by Raymond Shum,
    execution by Terry Aaron Wong
Interior design by Typesmith

Talonbooks acknowledges the financial support of the Canada Council for the
Arts, the Government of Canada through the Canada Book Fund, and the Province
of British Columbia through the British Columbia Arts Council and the Book
Publishing Tax Credit.

Rights to produce *1 Hour Photo*, in whole or in part, in any medium by any group,
amateur or professional, are retained by the author. Interested persons are requested
to apply to Tetsuro Shigematsu care of Talonbooks.

LIBRARY AND ARCHIVES CANADA CATALOGUING IN PUBLICATION

Shigematsu, Tetsuro, author
    1 hour photo / Tetsuro Shigematsu ; foreword by the family of Midge and
Karl Ayukawa ; introduction by Naomi Yamamoto ; afterword by Joy Kogawa.

A play.
ISBN 978-1-77201-215-6 (SOFTCOVER)

    I. Title. II. Title: One hour photo.
PS8637.H522A63 2018        C812'.6        C2018-904189-7

For Bahareh

If I had met you, and we parted ways, you would have been my Midge – the one I could never forget.

Instead, you became my Joan – the one I cannot live without.

Character, like a photograph, develops in darkness.

—YOUSUF KARSH

# Contents

## Our Mother, Midge

Tetsuro Shigematsu contacted us in the summer of 2017 when he heard about a photo album our mother had kept. He told us that our mother was one of the characters in a play he was writing that portrayed the role she had played in the life of Mas, his main protagonist. He wanted to know more about her.

Our mother was born in Vancouver in 1930 and, as a member of the Japanese Canadian community during World War II, was interned at Lemon Creek along with her mother, father, and three brothers. She later became a research scientist, a mother, a wife, and a historian who dedicated her final years to collecting Issei and Nisei stories and sharing the history of the internment camps.

Our mother created a photo album that chronicled her life from a young child in Vancouver to the start of her professional life at the National Research Council Canada. Recognizing the album's historical importance, she carefully recorded the names and dates of the images within. After she died, our family donated it to the Canadian War Museum so the collection would be available to scholars and to the general public, and so it would be properly preserved and catalogued. There are photographs of Mas – whom my mother met in the camp – in the album, which prove its personal as well as academic significance. In the end, Tetsuro used some of Midge's photos in his production and we are pleased to see them used in this way.

Our mother passed away in 2013 and since then we have met many people – her old friends, Nisei, historians, and human rights advocates – who have each revealed a different facet of her life. It is wonderful to know that she touched so many so significantly and with such altruism. We think she would be pleased that Tetsuro Shigematsu is bringing the story of the internment camps to a new audience.

As a family, we recognize that history and storytelling differ in purpose and in the way they treat facts and personalities. Nevertheless, Tetsuro Shigematsu has created a beautiful tribute to Mas in his play, and has shown how political events and personal actions combine to shape an individual's destiny. Thank you, Mas, for sharing your stories, and thank you, Tetsuro Shigematsu, for dramatizing them.

—THE FAMILY OF MIDGE AND KARL AYUKAWA

# Questions We Never Think to Ask Our Fathers

How many of us have asked our parents such questions as "Who was your first love?" or "What might have been your darkest hour?"

Thanks to an incredible effort by Tetsuro Shigematsu – writer, radio broadcaster, actor, and father – I have answers to these and other questions that I never thought to ask my father, Mas Yamamoto.

These things I do know about my father: he enjoys playing golf and blackjack; he's an angler; he's independent, stubborn, highly critical, curious, intelligent, thrifty; he doesn't like to eat lamb; and he doesn't like his full given name, Masanobu. He raised three children and he loved my mother, Joan. He has had to reinvent himself several times, sometimes out of necessity, sometimes because of war, boredom, and family considerations. He didn't always like who he had to become, but he always found the courage to change.

Mas was born in 1927 in Steveston, British Columbia, a small fishing village at the time, in an area called Vancouver Cannery located on the southwest corner of Sea Island. He didn't learn to speak English until he started school, having spent his first five or six years speaking only Japanese in a predominantly tight-knit Japanese immigrant community on the banks of the Fraser River. As a young teenager, he, his recently widowed mother, and his siblings became known as Enemy Aliens. His family, along with twenty-one thousand other Japanese Canadians, were forced to leave their homes with only the belongings they could carry in one suitcase each.

Canada was at war. Lemon Creek Internment Camp was Mas' home for the next four years.

Mas' new home was a hastily erected shack, identical to those of all the other interned families, built row upon row, providing little protection from the frigid Kootenay winters and affording no privacy. His education was cut short until classrooms were built – but only for elementary school-age children, and Mas was fifteen years old at the time. Of course, freedom of movement was curtailed. It wasn't all bad. Mas has fond memories of playing baseball, boxing, and getting into mischief with his friends. He recalls that his mother felt the trauma of the internment much more than he did as a young teenager.

Mas' childhood ended abruptly following his release from the internment camp. He had to support his mother and siblings by working long days in a fruit orchard in the Okanagan, and this meant he couldn't pursue his education or any of the other things he had longed to do after his incarceration.

It was Tetsuro who asked my father the question, "What was your darkest hour?" In response, Mas revealed the depths of his despair following the war when he considered ending his own life, and that story is told in *1 Hour Photo*. I was stunned, then saddened, to hear my dad's recorded voice recount the motivating incident in his quiet, dignified manner. I was also slightly amused to hear him tell the story in his typically matter-of-fact way, using a tone more consistent with deciding which socks to wear that day.

Tetsuro had lost his dad just a few months before he began his interviews with my father. Tetsuro's highly successful play, *Empire of the Son*, explored uneasy tensions in the relationship between him, a hip, contemporary navigator of Western pop culture, and his emotionally constrained Japanese immigrant father. Tetsuro's dad, Akira Shigematsu, died just two weeks before the play's premiere. Perhaps Tetsuro needed to continue that conversation, but this time he began to talk with my dad. For this, my sister Donna and my brother Brian and I owe Tetsuro a debt of gratitude. He has closely examined the uncomfortable distance that often appears in the relationships between traditional Asian Canadian fathers and their children.

Mas had always challenged us. My mother nurtured, fed, cared for, and clothed us, but Mas pressed us to learn more. Our road trips were filled with pop quizzes. When we wrote letters to him while he worked in New York, he returned them with the grammar corrected. Education was always a priority in our household. Mas had completed his high school matriculation, bachelor's, and master's in record time. When I was six years old, my dad received his PhD – at thirty-eight years old. We were raised thinking that we had no choice but to attend university.

Following our post-secondary educations, my sister and brother both owned and operated their own businesses, as did I. Mas, too, became an entrepreneur when he left the academic research world and reinvented himself once again. Eventually my father and mother owned and operated three Japan Camera 1 Hour Photo franchises. Tetsuro embarked on the conversations with Mas and the journey of discovery that is *1 Hour Photo* after noticing several Japan Camera 1 Hour Photo artifacts at my sister's house, including a coffee mug and a set of towels. Always curious and questioning, he began to speak with my father and developed an easy rapport that I envy to this day.

As a fourth-generation Canadian, the internment had no direct impact upon me, yet I've had an abiding curiosity about it for my entire life. In elementary school, I took the identity card that my father had been required to carry under the War Measures Act and used it as part of a school project.

Always deeply respectful of my elders, I felt a need to raise awareness of their stories. In 1949, Canadians of Japanese descent were finally given the right to vote and, in 2008, I was honoured to be the first Japanese Canadian to be elected as a Member of the Legislative Assembly in British Columbia. In 2012, Tosh Suzuki approached me to introduce a Motion of Apology. This motion, supported by all parties, served to apologize for the actions of a former B.C. government, seventy years after the unjust internment of so many Canadians of Japanese descent. My father was in the gallery to witness this event.

Tetsuro is a gifted raconteur. You will enjoy this story and take away its many ideas of forgiveness and the lessons of history. The one I heard loudest was to ask our parents the unasked questions. I invite you to ask your father, "Who was your first love?" You may be surprised. I don't know if my father has a favourite colour. There are still more questions to ask.

This year my dad turned ninety-one. I wonder how he'll reinvent himself next ...

—NAOMI YAMAMOTO

## Playwright's Note

The award-winning style of *1 Hour Photo* began, like all great relationships, in a bar. During our run of *Empire of the Son* – my previous solo work – at the National Arts Centre in Ottawa, Susan Miyagishima and I were decompressing post-show at Deacon Brodie's Pub on bustling Elgin Street. I was swiping through the photo album on her smart phone (such is the casual intimacy of touring life), and I recall being struck by the photos of the knitted creations she made for her niece: a pumpkin hat, a strawberry toque. Her culinary millinery was so intricate, so beautifully constructed, I had one of those impulses that smarter people consider for a moment, then file away for further rumination, but not me. Immediately, I asked, "Susan, how would you feel about making the miniatures for my next show?" Her response was pure Miyagishima. Her eyes widened, and her fingers danced beneath her chin like over-stimulated sea anemones. And so it was decided. Not only would Susan be stage managing *1 Hour Photo*, but she would have the additional responsibility of crafting the miniatures.

In *Empire of the Son*, the autobiographical solo work that I wrote and continue to perform and tour, we developed a visual style that struck a chord with audiences. Onstage, I focus a camera at miniature objects I manipulate, and this live footage is then projected onto a movie screen for audiences to see. This technique was developed in response to a question I asked. Because *Empire of the Son* is a show that involves radio, how could we deepen the experience of listening? Consider why campfire stories are so captivating. Is it because ghost stories have exceptional narrative powers? Or is it because the experience of being hemmed in by darkness, coupled by the mesmerizing dance of flames, provides the ideal distraction to enable deeply imaginative listening? Within the darkened setting of a theatre, what would be the visual equivalent of staring into hypnotic flames? The answer was magnifying the tiny.

What is it about miniatures that we find so engrossing? All things tiny seem to be part of the zeitgeist. If I asked you, "Hey, do you wanna watch a video of doughnuts being deep fried?" you'd likely decline. But when that doughnut is no bigger than a single Cheerio, that video will go viral. I personally subscribe to @tanaka_tatsuya's Instagram account. This Japanese artist places miniature figures onto household objects with such wit, he transforms the quotidian into epic mise-en-scène.

I imagine an artist like Tatsuya must walk around the world with a very particular lens, forever looking at how the very small might represent the very large. When I was interviewing Mas Yamamoto, I remember him telling me about how his father died all alone on his fishing boat. On a personal level, I was haunted. But as a theatre artist, I wondered, how can I represent that onstage?

FOUND OBJECTS

When I was staying over at my friend Troy's home, his son Joshua was kind enough to lend me his room for the night. A twelve-year-old boy's bedroom is a shrine to the gods of wonder. His walls were covered with posters of pro motor-cycle riders. His carpet was strewn with the detritus of half-destroyed Lego spaceships. Next to his window was a wooden model of a fishing vessel whose hull alone was about the size of a breadbox. I could see that the wooden decks were just big enough to accommodate a wireless GoPro camera.

If I placed the boat/camera upon a lazy Susan, and it was lit with a special that simulated moonlight, it was easy to imagine how the mast and rigging would cast eerie shadows that would sweep across the ship's bow again and again. The sound of an actual wooden fishing vessel creaking upon the lapping ocean would complete the hypnotic effect, as the audience listened to Mas' weathered voice describe the moment of his father's death.

No kid likes to part with a beloved toy, so when I asked Joshua (and his mom and dad) if I could "borrow" it for my show, I made my verbal quotation marks extra clear. Having commandeered my children's toys as the miniatures for *Empire of the Son* (but accused of much worse), I wanted to make it absolutely clear, before he assented, that he shouldn't expect his boat back until well after his voice broke. Joshua cheerfully shrugged and laughed at me the way he usually does.

I rode home on the SkyTrain, with the boat cradled in my arms, feeling euphoric. This is the life of a vagabond theatre artist. We give ourselves peculiar problems to solve, only to find solutions in the most unexpected places. We beg, borrow, and steal, then make out like bandits.

SOURCED OBJECTS

One of the privileges of being an artistic master within the Renaissance tradition is being able to come up with ideas and have your apprentices execute them. Sadly, this is not my situation, but that does not stop me from pretending it is. One thing I realized while creating this show is that, as long as I live, I will never venture further out into the world than when my parents first emigrated from Japan. Back then, the world was so much larger. It took so much imagination, such courage, it is hard for me to fathom. To undertake a comparable journey, I would have to venture into space. As a playwright, I decided to bookend Mas' life story by talking about Voyager, NASA's legendary 1970s space program. As far as spacecraft go, the Voyager probe is very weird looking. If a satellite dish and a construction crane had a love child, it would look like Voyager. As pleasurable as it may be for you to read my description here on the page, I knew a live audience would prefer just to see the damn thing. So how about projecting a Creative Commons–licensed image of Voyager onto that beautiful, gigantic blank-photograph-waiting-to-be-developed projection screen designed by our award-winning set designer Pam Johnson? Maybe have it animated in Adobe After Effects by our award-winning video designer Jamie Nesbit? No. Oftentimes simplest is best. I'll just show it to the audience like it's show-and-tell. Of course that's easy for me to say. "Ahem. Oh Susan? Could you please build this Hasegawa 1:48 plastic scale model of the Voyager space probe I just happen to have in my briefcase because I ordered it via two-day shipping from Amazon? No rush."

### BESPOKE OBJECTS

Some scale models simply can't be sourced online. Like a rough-hewn bunk bed, the kind the government of British Columbia quickly assembled by the hundreds to accommodate the forced displacement of Canadians of Japanese descent from their homes. The instructions to the head carpenter was probably something along the lines of "Make 'em quick, make 'em cheap, but not so cheap that they'll collapse. We don't wanna be providing no medical care for them Japs." No matter how many dollhouse inventories I could source, how would I ever find a bunk bed with coarse-enough textures to reflect the roughness of this historical injustice? I couldn't. But Susan understood what they needed to look like without my even having to explain. What's more, she also sewed pillows and bedding that were historically accurate.

So what exactly do I bring to the equation? It was my idea to place this bunk bed into a semitransparent box of two-way mirrors, so the audience could see them multiplied – the way they went on forever in the Forum building at Hastings Park. But guess who constructed the funhouse mirror box? You guessed it. Some of you may think I'm writing this with Susan looking over my shoulder, but you'd be wrong. She does watch over me, but only in a good way. The kind of way that results in Vancouver Asian Canadian Theatre's first Jessie Award for Significant Artistic Achievement, Small Theatre – Tetsuro Shigematsu, Jamie Nesbitt, and Susan Miyagishima – *1 Hour Photo* – Vancouver Asian Canadian Theatre – outstanding technical design and execution for the purpose of historical storytelling.

According to the jurors, "The emotional impact of the story (historical injustice) was sharply enhanced by these visuals" allowing the audience to "situate themselves at the site of the story." And that's how you create art that resonates. Keep your ego in check and work with people who are better than you. Oh yes, and one more thing. Find the story of a lifetime worth sharing with the world. Thank you for sharing yours with me, Mas.

—TETSURO SHIGEMATSU

(*above*) Tetsuro and Steve guide the GoPro camera across the semitransparent box of two-way mirrors, creating the illusion of infinite bunk beds.

(*below*) Tetsuro spins the lazy Susan with scale-model fishing boat, causing shadows to sweep across the wooden decks. The action is captured by a wireless GoPro mounted on the ship's bow.

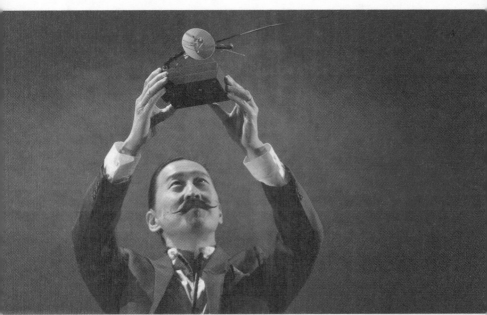

(*above*) The Voyager space probe is a marvel of engineering, but so is the magnetic, illuminated, battery-powered scale model designed by aerospace engineer Susan Miyagashima.

(*below*) Although appearing simple, a camera move like this requires considerable gluteal isometric strength!

*All photos on pages xxiv–xxv by Raymond Shum.*

## Production History

*1 Hour Photo* was first produced by Vancouver Asian Canadian Theatre and developed with the assistance of Playwrights Theatre Centre. It was presented in the Historic Theatre at The Cultch in Vancouver, from October 3 to 15, 2017, with the following cast and crew:

| | |
|---|---|
| PERFORMER, WRITER & FILMMAKER | Tetsuro Shigematsu |
| PERFORMER, SOUND DESIGNER & COMPOSER | Steve Charles |
| ARTISTIC PRODUCER | Donna Yamamoto |
| DIRECTOR | Richard Wolfe |
| DRAMATURG | Heidi Taylor |
| SET DESIGNER | Pam Johnson |
| LIGHTING DESIGNER | Gerald King |
| COSTUME DESIGNER | Laura Fukumoto |
| COSTUME DESIGN MENTOR | Barbara Clayden |
| AUDIO DRAMATURG | Yvonne Gall |
| VIDEO DESIGNER | Jamie Nesbitt |
| TECHNICAL DIRECTOR & PRODUCTION MANAGER | Adrian Muir |
| STAGE MANAGER & DESIGNER OF MODELS & MINIATURES | Susan Miyagishima |
| APPRENTICE STAGE MANAGER | Maria Zarrillo |
| APPRENTICE LIGHTING DESIGNER | Tory Ip |

# Characters

All characters are played by TETSURO, with slight shifts of physicality and voice. He periodically interacts with STEVE who appears on stage to perform musical accompaniment. Audio and video recordings of MAS and other characters are seen and heard during the performance or appear as offstage voices.

# 1 HOUR PHOTO

(*above*) Production shot of stage set with upstage shelves, musical instruments and two plinths (one for the turntable and one for the lazy Susan) stage left, and a third plinth for the scale-model house downstage right. *Raymond Shum*.

(*below*) Production shot of Tetsuro holding up the transparent vinyl record of interviews with Mas. *Raymond Shum*.

*A large projection screen, four metres wide and three metres tall, dominates the upper stage. It is framed with a white border, suggesting an enormous undeveloped instant-print photograph. It is held in place by four triangular photo-mounting corner tabs – the kind one would find in an old photo album.*

*Beneath this enormous blank photograph / projection screen is a long set of drawers and shelves. The shelves hold lidded boxes and groups of small objects of a scientific nature, such as a globe, chemistry flasks, and the scale model of a wooden fishing boat.*

*Stage left is a waist-high plinth that supports a lazy Susan. The plinth has a hidden shelf that holds several objects to be used during the performance. Also stage left, a turntable is set on another waist-high plinth, and a couple of electronic keyboards and a guitar amp await the arrival of STEVE, the composer and musician.*

*Stage right is a scale model of the house at 665 Royal Road set on a third waist-high plinth. The scale model is open at the top so that TETSURO* can reach in to use his fingers to create "fingerplays" of the action described. TETSURO operates a GoPro camera mounted on a selfie stick to create live videos of the fingerplay both in the scale-model house and on the lazy Susan.

Live video from the GoPro camera as well as recorded videos and still images are projected onto the upstage screen.

PROJECTION:
VIDEO with STILL IMAGES of the ideograms 日 ("Nihon" meaning "Japan") and 系 ("keitō" or "lineage") alternate with a STILL IMAGE showing their English equivalent: "Nikkei: a Canadian of Japanese descent."

## Voyager

*STEVE enters stage left. He wears jeans and
a tweed brown vest over a white band-collar
button-up shirt with rolled-up sleeves. He carries
a vintage hollow-body electric jazz guitar and
attends to his music station: a couple of electronic
keyboards, a guitar amp, and an array of foot
pedals. TETSURO enters stage left. He wears a
close-fitting blue suit, a white shirt with brown
leather detailing, and vintage brown leather
suspenders. He crosses to STEVE. During the stage
manager's front-of-house speech, they quietly chat
together; then TETSURO crosses to centre stage.
With a big physical movement, he cues STEVE.*

*SOUND:*
*STEVE plays a funked-up blues riff*
*that explodes into the space.*

*Snap. Stage lights up.*

(*over music*) The year is 1977. The place, planet Earth. And even
though some of you were not yet born, believe me when I say
it was a very cool time in which to be alive. Me? I was a little
kid. And some of the things you know and love today were just
being introduced. A movie named *Star Wars* came out. The US
Department of Defense launched a series of satellites you know as
GPS. 1977 was the year the Apple II went on sale – you wouldn't
have wanted the Apple I. It was made of wood. Seriously! – Back
then, the Prime Minister was Trudeau. And in New York City,
they were putting the finishing touches on a pair of buildings they
christened the World Trade Center.

But for my money, the coolest thing to launch in 1977 was one of the first digital cameras. It was the size of a Volkswagen Beetle if you can believe it, but the cool thing is what they named it. "Voyager."

> *TETSURO produces a scale model*
> *of the Voyager space probe and places*
> *it on the waist-high lazy Susan.*

Its mission? To take a Family Portrait: a series of photographs of the outer planets of our solar system.

> *The funky music crescendos, as TETSURO*
> *does a robotic dance while miming the taking*
> *of a photograph. The music slows down like*
> *a turntable losing power, and TETSURO'S*
> *animatronic persona "dies" on its feet.*

For all our technologies, all our miraculous gadgets, when it comes to the things we wish to keep, we regularly experience catastrophic loss. According to archivists, the best way to preserve an important document is to print it out. Ink on paper is the only way to ensure a unique arrangement of words will endure. Alternatively, clay tablets seem to display some longevity as well. As for sound, if you want to preserve the dulcet tones of your beloved, how do you do that?

> *TETSURO turns away from the audience as*
> *his voice seamlessly transitions from live to*
> *recorded. As the audio continues, TETSURO*
> *picks up a clear glass mug from inside the scale*
> *model of the house, turns upstage, and takes a*
> *long sip of water. As he turns back to face the*
> *audience while still drinking, it becomes clear that*
> *Tetsuro's seemingly live voice is in fact a recording.*
> *With a wink, he places the cup of water on the*
> *upstage shelves beneath the projection screen.*

*SOUND:*
*AUDIO CLIP of Tetsuro's voice.*

TETSURO: (*recorded*) This question of how to best preserve a voice has been a preoccupation for our team of artists because our show is based on thirty-six hours' worth of recorded interviews – from one person. Don't worry, we won't be playing you all thirty-six hours.

> *Tetsuro's voice goes live as he finishes*
> *drinking and continues to speak.*

Oh no, to tell the story of a life, we had the audacity to select just eighteen minutes. That's a ratio of more than a hundred to one if you're curious, and we have taken those eighteen minutes, mastered them, and pressed them into vinyl. You can find custom record plants online pretty easily these days. It only costs about a hundred dollars, but if taken care of properly, and by "properly" I mean sticking it on a shelf, that record will outlast all of us. But what about pressing a record that will outlast all of humankind? The man who accomplished that feat was named Carl Sagan.

Now for those of you who don't know who Carl Sagan is, he's kind of like Neil deGrasse Tyson's white father. A towering public intellectual, and the host of the PBS-TV show *Cosmos* – the first one. So Carl and company composed a message for aliens, mastered it on a golden record, mounted that record onto the side of that Volkswagon-sized camera, bolted the whole assembly on top of a Titan II rocket, and lit that candle. A message in a bottle flung into the ocean of space.

> *TETSURO moves stage left and spins*
> *the lazy Susan. The scale-model Voyager*
> *rotates in its own spotlight.*

*SOUND:*
*STEVE responds musically with space-*
*themed music that continues under.*

But for all the poetry of the gesture, the contents of the record itself are remarkably banal. It contains greetings in fifty-five different languages. Which sounds like a good idea, right? But it comes off sounding like a bad radio spot for Rosetta Stone. I once listened to the entire album on SoundCloud. Bach and Beethoven interspersed with an eclectic selection of world music.

It felt a lot like listening to *CBC Radio Overnight*. And I suppose that's the problem with the record. It's a little bland. It sounds like it was put together by committee, because it was. Now, I think it would have been far better if they included the voice of just one person on that record. Have one person tell their story. And by telling just one person's story, you're going to get a lot closer to shining a light on what it is to be human than *bonjour, buenos días, konnichi wa.*

*TETSURO lifts the Voyager model off the rotating*
*lazy Susan and "flies" it to the upstage shelves.*

The challenge is, no matter who you choose, that one person will be completely wrong for nearly everyone. Well, I'm not on a committee, and the person I've chosen is kind of like me. He's a "Nikkei." Don't worry, this is the only vocabulary you are going to learn.

TETSURO: Steve?

STEVE: Yes, Tetsuro.

TETSURO: What is a "Nikkei"?

STEVE: A Canadian of Japanese descent.

TETSURO: For example?

STEVE: Like yourself, Tetsuro.

TETSURO: (*to audience*) Yes, Steve. I am *also* a Nikkei – a Canadian of Japanese descent, but more importantly so is Mas Yamamoto.

> *On the word "Yamamoto," TETSURO raises both hands to illustrate the ideogram for "mountain,"* 山.

My chosen one.

> *STEVE delivers a transparent vinyl record to TETSURO at centre stage.*
>
> *SOUND:*
> *AUDIO CLIP of Aaron Copland's* Fanfare for the Common Man (1942).
>
> *TETSURO holds the record high above his head in a pin spot before placing it on the turntable stage left. STEVE drops the needle. TETSURO perches on a stool downstage centre while the AUDIO plays under. STEVE returns to the musical instruments stage left.*
>
> *Lights fade down.*

~

## Dirty Photos

*Lights fade up.*

*SOUND:*
*RECORD TRACK of MAS sharing*
*a story about the early days of film*
*processing for different customers.*

MAS: (*recorded*) When we first started the business in Capilano Mall, a lady approached me. "Do you develop and print sensitive photos?" And I assumed that she was referring to, say, films – 400 ASA films – which are very light sensitive. So I said, "No problem." And when the pictures came out, they were – there was a man and a woman and they were both naked. And she was also pregnant. And he was, or she was bending in front of him – on her knees! Now I don't think I can be much more graphic than that. It is almost embarrassing to even talk about it. I am kind of a prudish guy, you know, but anyways, it was an education for me. But in those days, you know – talking about the eighties – who knows what we might have faced, printing so-called dirty pictures? Oh my God. Nowadays, I wouldn't call those pictures "obscene" but they were certainly eye openers. Ah yes.

> *Lights reveal the scale model of a suburban*
> *home downstage right. It is Tetsuro's home at*
> *665 Royal Road. TETSURO walks over.*

This is where I live, and the reason why this place is important for our purposes here tonight is because this is where I interviewed the man of the hour, Mas Yamamoto.

> *TETSURO moves behind the scale-model*
> *home and produces a selfie stick, which he*
> *displays to the audience. Attached to the*
> *end of the selfie stick is a small camera.*

GoPro.

> *Using the selfie stick, TETSURO inserts*
> *the GoPro into the scale-model home*
> *and presses the Record button.*

> *PROJECTION:*
> *LIVE VIDEO of the miniature dining room*
> *within the scale-model home appears.*

> *TETSURO reaches into the back of the scale-*
> *model house and picks up a tiny object.*

Every week, we sat down here at this table.

> *PROJECTION:*
> *LIVE VIDEO of Tetsuro's gigantic*
> *hand carefully placing two tiny glasses*
> *of tea on the miniature table.*

"Mondays with Mas," 10:00 a.m. We always booked just an hour, but we tended to go much longer.

> *PROJECTION:*
> *LIVE VIDEO of Tetsuro's hand as he places*
> *a tiny microphone complete with stand*
> *and cable onto the dining room table.*

> STEVE: Man, Tetsuro! How come you're hanging out with this old guy so much? He's like ninety years old, right? Isn't that kind of weird, man? Is it because you're missing your dad?

11

TETSURO: (*to STEVE*) The truth is, I don't know. It's a puzzle to me.

(*to audience*) "Mas" is short for "Masanobu." The ideogram for his name means "first to charge." "Tetsuro" means "philosophical young man." And I suppose that sums up our relationship. Mas has always been the archetypal warrior in the battlefield of life, fighting against all odds, and I'm just the curious scribe asking him questions as I ponder philosophy's most basic question, "How does one live?"

*TETSURO crosses to centre stage.*

I first met Mas because I'm friends with his daughter, Donna Yamamoto, who is also my boss. Anyone here have a boss? Can you imagine living in your boss's house? It's a little weird, right? To this day, I still find myself asking, how did I end up living in such a beautiful house? Recently, there was a season in my life that was pretty stormy. Donna, being the good friend she is, asked me –

*SOUND:*
*AUDIO CLIP of DONNA inviting TETSURO*
*to live in her family home at 665 Royal Road.*

DONNA: (*recorded*) How can I help?

TETSURO: (*live*) Help me find a place big enough so my parents can move in with me.

DONNA: (*recorded*) Why don't you take mine?

TETSURO: (*live*) What? Uh, thank you but no.

DONNA: (*recorded*) I mean it, you guys should move into my place.

(*to audience*) So I did. Now when you move into someone else's home – like doing Airbnb – no matter how clean they leave it for you, they can't help but leave behind so many clues. For me, it was *this* that piqued my curiosity.

> *TETSURO pulls the Japan Camera mug*
> *out of the scale model of 665 Royal Road*
> *and walks it over to the lazy Susan. STEVE*
> *aims the GoPro camera at the mug.*

What was my friend Donna's connection to this franchise I could scarcely remember?

> *PROJECTION:*
> *LIVE VIDEO of a white porcelain mug*
> *being placed in front of the GoPro on the*
> *lazy Susan. As it rotates, the red and yellow*
> *Japan Camera logo comes into view.*
>
> *TETSURO retrieves the Japan Camera*
> *mug and gestures to it as he speaks.*

Over his life, Mas has played a lot of different roles, but in the eighties, he was a businessman, a franchise operator who owned several Japan Camera stores, which were a chain of one-hour photofinishing labs.

I know that, for some of you, one-hour photos were before your time, so let me just take a moment to impress upon you that, back in the day, you had to wait a whole day, or even weeks, to get your photos back. So when one-hour photos came along, that was a huge breakthrough. Today of course the notion of having to wait a full hour to see your photos? Unacceptable!

And as I listened to Mas, I learned a thing or two about the world of one-hour photo finishing. For example, did you know it was a seasonal business? Anyone care to guess when business was busiest?

> TETSURO *interacts with the audience,*
> *hearing their guesses about which season*
> *was busiest for film processing.*

Traffic would peak late August, early September, because by then you had a whole summer's worth of memories ready to be developed.

> PROJECTION:
> *VIDEO of DONNA and CUSTOMER in*
> *silhouette. The CUSTOMER approaches*
> *DONNA at the counter and pulls from*
> *his pockets roll after roll of exposed film*
> *canisters. He reluctantly hands them over.*

Mas told me there would often be a moment of hesitation as the customer was handing over their rolls film as in, "Wait a sec ... what's on this roll? What was I doing that made someone yell, 'Quick! Get the camera! Get the camera!'" These thoughts would flicker behind their eyes, as in, "You're going to see all my photos. Are you going to judge me? Make doubles? Betray my trust in you?" And I couldn't help but think maybe Mas was having similar thoughts over the course of our thirty-six hours together. "These are my memories. What are you going to do with them?"

> TETSURO *takes a scale-model fishing boat from*
> *the shelf. It has a GoPro preset on the bow. He*
> *places the boat on the lazy Susan and rotates it.*

> SOUND:
> *STEVE drops the needle on the record*
> *player, and then plays quiet musical*
> *accompaniment under the audio recording.*

(*above*) Production shot of GoPro image of rotating scale-model fishing boat. *Raymond Shum.*

(*below*) Fishermen's Reserve rounding up Japanese Canadian fishing vessels at Anniedale Dyke on December 10, 1941. *Library and Archives Canada, PA-037467.*

*PROJECTION:*
*LIVE VIDEO of fishing boat rotating.*
*Close-up of the boat's interior and the shadows*
*cast by the mast as the boat rotates.*

*SOUND:*
*AUDIO CLIP of boat creaking.*

*SOUND:*
*RECORD TRACK of MAS describing*
*his father's fishing boat found turning in*
*circles off the coast of Vancouver Island.*

MAS: (*recorded*) I don't really know a heck of a lot about
him. You know, just because he passed away, you know,
when I was about fourteen, I think, thirteen or fourteen. Of
course my dad, being a fisherman, was on his boat off the
coast of Vancouver Island. It was only – because – people
in those days, the fishermen, the Japanese fishermen, they
used to fish in groups – that a friend notices his boat was
going around in circles, and knew there was something
wrong. So checked, and my dad was in the cabin. There
was blood all over. I think he died of a perforated gastric
ulcer, a large artery in the stomach lining, and when that,
the hemorrhage starts, you know, just bled to death, was
helpless really.

*TETSURO "scratches" the vinyl record a*
*couple of times to repeat the phrase.*

MAS: (*recorded*) … was helpless really … was helpless
really.

*TETSURO moves back to the scale*
*model of the house at 665 Royal Road*
*and reactivates the GoPro camera.*

*PROJECTION:*
*RECORDED VIDEO of the interior walls*
*at 665 Royal Road as they transform into*
*the Yamamoto family home in Vancouver,*
*before the war. A portrait of Mas' father,*
*Toraichi, slowly appears on the wall, next*
*to a portrait of his mother, Yasu.*

*SOUND:*
*RECORD TRACK of MAS remembering*
*the community members who visited*
*his mother with the news.*

MAS: (*recorded*) Well I remember these people. As I say, I can't remember. At least there were two – there might have been as many as three or four – walked into the house. My mother was there of course. I was standing at the doorway of the living room. The word that the father had died. Yeah, there was almost a – like a thunderclap in my ears. Just a, yeah, a thunderclap I guess. Except very sharp. Hard to explain. I can't even understand, even myself, why I didn't go to my mother. Instead, I turned my back and left the doorway, and left into the kitchen area by myself. I don't know why.

*TETSURO lifts the needle off the record.*

*PROJECTION:*
*VIDEO of the two black-and-white*
*portraits of Mas' parents, Toraichi and*
*Yasu, as they fill the entire screen.*

*TETSURO raises the fishing boat*
*and presents it to the audience.*

As far as deaths go, this is not the one you want: all alone, at work, in pain, and worried. As Mas' father was dying, I'll bet his last thoughts were about his kids: Emiko, Sam, Hiromu, Mas, Tomiharu, Hamako, Midori, and Tatsuo. Who was going to help his wife, Yasu, raise their seven kids?

> *PROJECTION:*
> *STILL IMAGE of Toraichi's portrait*
> *disappears, leaving only an empty frame.*
> *Yasu's picture-bride portrait remains.*

As he closed his eyes for the last time on his fishing boat, little did he know that there were such thunderclouds gathering beyond the horizon. Mas' father died on July 4, 1941, five months before Pearl Harbor. Maybe he was lucky he didn't live to see the day. When Japanese Zeros dropped their bombs on the American fleet in Hawaii, the shockwave travelled all the way across the Pacific Ocean and swept away an entire community into the heart of B.C. like a tsunami. The family would never be the same again.

> *Lights shift.*

> *SOUND:*
> *STEVE plays a series of hallucinogenic*
> *electric guitar chords.*

# Infinity

*TETSURO spins 360 degrees on one
heel and stops, facing STEVE.*

When a school child multiplies ten times ten, *that* is mathematics.
When Michael Bay multiplies Transformers, that is CGI. But when
Steve and I multiply objects here on stage, *this* is smoke and mirrors.

*In the manner of a Las Vegas magician,
TETSURO produces a semitransparent box of
two-way mirrors and places it on the lazy Susan.*

*SOUND:
STEVE continues to play hallucinogenic chords
on his electric guitar; then pauses and speaks.*

STEVE: Well maybe not smoke, Tetsuro.

TETSURO: No, but mirrors.

STEVE: In fact, two-way mirrors.

TETSURO: A *box* of two-way mirrors.

*TETSURO spins the mirror box on top of
the lazy Susan and places his hand inside.
As it rotates, the audience can see Tetsuro's
hand multiplied in an infinity mirror effect.*

TETSURO: Hey, Steve, have you ever seen so many
wedding bands in your life?

STEVE: It's terrifying.

TETSURO: Spoken like a true bachelor.

> *TETSURO withdraws his hand, goes to*
> *the upstage shelves, opens a drawer, and*
> *picks up a miniature wooden bunk bed.*

A bunk bed is a wonderful thing: the magic carpet adventure of the top bunk, the cave-like coziness of the bottom. Unless, of course, you're an adult. If you're a man or a woman and you find yourself weighing the pros and cons of top bunk versus bottom, that's a pretty good indication something has gone horribly wrong with your life.

> *TETSURO places the wooden bunk bed*
> *into the mirror box. TETSURO grabs the*
> *selfie stick with GoPro and begins shooting*
> *a tracking shot across the bunk beds.*

> *PROJECTION:*
> *LIVE VIDEO shows the one bunk bed*
> *multiplied an infinite number of times.*

After Pearl Harbor, thousands of Japanese Canadians had their homes seized by the government. They had just twenty-four hours to pack up what they could carry, and then they found themselves being corralled on the grounds of Vancouver's county fair, the PNE at Hastings Park.

> *PROJECTION:*
> *LIVE VIDEO of the mirror box with*
> *bunk beds merges into a black-and-white*
> *archival photo of bunk beds in the men's*
> *dormitory at Hastings Park, 1942.*

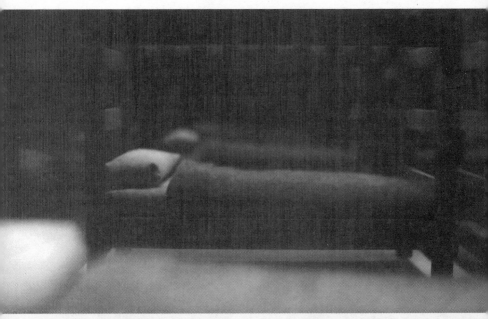

(*above*) GoPro image of bunk beds reflected row upon row in the mirror box. *Tetsuro Shigematsu.*

(*below*) Men's dormitory in Forum building, Building K, during Japanese Canadian internment and relocation, 1942. *City of Vancouver Archives / Pacific National Exhibition Fonds AM281-S8-: CVA 180-354.*

This is the PNE Forum – maybe you've enjoyed a concert here – it was designated as the men's dormitory. Police were stationed at the entrances to guard against wives and girlfriends entering the space to prevent, and I quote, "further propagation of the species." Women and children were housed in the Livestock Building, where they had all the creature comforts of farm animals.

> *TETSURO removes the bunk bed from the*
> *mirror box and places it on the upstage shelves.*
> *He moves downstage centre and listens.*

> *SOUND:*
> *RECORD TRACK of Mas' reflections.*

MAS: (*recorded*) I used to think about – what is the difference between dying and living? Obviously we know when a person is no longer living but, you know, the hair grows, the cells in your body will continue going until they eventually run out of energy, and when all the biochemical reactions reach equilibrium – nothing else happening – is that person dead? I think there is physics term called entropy, the point where there is no more reaction of any kind, the sum of all activity is zero.

I was never the best son, but thanks to my friend Donna, when the sandstorms of death began blowing, I got to play genie, and grant my father's dying wish, which was to die at home. Sounds simple, right? It wasn't. At the time, my parents were living in a concrete shoebox in the West End. My dad didn't want to die in a high-rise. He didn't want to die in a hospital, behind a curtain in palliative care. He wanted to die at home. And by "home" I mean that in the Norman Rockwell sense of the term, with his wife, one of his children, and his grandchildren. Three generations in one house, in a place big enough to shelter this extended family through inclement weather – a place like 665 Royal Road.

*STEVE operates the camera while TETSURO*
*places miniature furniture in the scale-model house.*

*PROJECTION:*
*LIVE VIDEO of GoPro tour of the scale-*
*model house at 665 Royal Road.*

Now my little family, we have always lived in super-small places. Basement suites, graduate housing. So when we first moved into 665, my kids were super excited by all the space; they ran from room to room, staking out their claims like little imperialists.

*PROJECTION:*
*LIVE VIDEO as TETSURO places a second*
*miniature bunk bed in the children's bedroom.*

This is the room I chose for my father. It's the smallest room in the house, no bigger than a walk-in closet, no windows, and his hospital bed would end up taking about half the space, but it does have one nice feature. A pair of French doors which opens out onto the balcony. As far as last rooms go, pretty damn good.

*PROJECTION:*
*VIDEO EFFECT showing the reflection of*
*evergreen trees in the glass of the French doors.*

At twelve hundred metres above sea level, it is nestled high among the rainforests of North Vancouver, where the oxygen is fragrant with the scent of cedar. If you're gonna take one last breath – hard to beat. In fact, it was around this time that I first met Donna's father, Mas. And I was so struck by his radiant health, because he was about the same age as my dad. Two Japanese men, same generation, but *so* different.

*TETSURO looks down in reflection.*

# Exile

*TETSURO pirouettes 360 degrees and stops,*
*facing the audience with renewed energy.*

Sociologists have noted that certain immigrant groups, despite having achieved economic stability here in Canada, keep on renting, even though they can afford a mortgage.

*STEVE places a stool centre stage*
*directly behind TETSURO.*

My father-in-law refused to sell his property in Iran. He used to fret, "What if the Canadian government kicks us out? Where will we go?" His kids would laugh at him. "Baba, this is Canada. That kind of thing does not happen here."

*TETSURO sits down on the stool.*

After Pearl Harbor in 1941, the Canadian government executed a to-do list against its own citizens that would have made Vladimir Putin proud.

*STEVE stands behind TETSURO, looming over*
*him like a threatening authority. With the aid of*
*a vocal processor, STEVE sounds like an old-time*
*AM radio announcer quoting government orders.*

STEVE: (*quoting*) Shut down community newspapers.

TETSURO: Check.

STEVE: (*quoting*) Every person of the Japanese race shall hereafter be at his usual place of residence each day before sunset and shall remain therein until sunrise on the following day.

TETSURO: Check.

STEVE: (*quoting*) No person of the Japanese race shall have in his possession any motor vehicle, radio transmitter, radio receiving set, or camera.

TETSURO: Check.

STEVE: (*quoting*) All Japanese mail and correspondence shall be censored.

TETSURO: Check.

STEVE: (*quoting*) All fishermen of the Japanese race shall hand over their fishing craft to the Custodian of Enemy Alien Property.

> *TETSURO has had enough. He jumps to his feet in protest, but stops when he sees the image onscreen.*

> *PROJECTION:*
> *STILL IMAGE of archival photo showing confiscated fishing boats at Anniedale Dyke on December 10, 1941. Library and Archives Canada, PA-037467.*

> *TETSURO stares defiantly out into the audience.*

≈

## Santa Barbara Tent

*TETSURO places the stool behind the scale*
*model of 665 Royal Road, then crosses to get*
*a miniature tent from the upstage shelves. He*
*places the miniature tent in the mirror box.*

I became a father on August 12, 2003. As a new parent you can't
help but remember dates like that, because there are so many
forms to fill out. Three years later, 2006, my little family is camping
in Santa Barbara, in the mountains next to this lake. It is the
middle of the night and my three-year-old daughter wakes up and
says, "I'm cold, Mommy." Without even opening her eyes, my wife
sweeps our three-year-old daughter into her own sleeping bag in
one motion. I roll over and nestle closer to them. Not for them,
but for me. I was scared. For some reason, those three words, "I'm
cold, Mommy," really frightened me. It was so cold. She was so
tiny. You never want your kid to be that cold.

*TETSURO grabs the selfie stick with*
*the GoPro and executes another tracking*
*shot across the mirror box.*

*PROJECTION:*
*LIVE VIDEO of mirror box with the*
*miniature tent multiplied many times over*
*merges into VIDEO of archival photos*
*showing rows of tents in Slocan City, 1942.*

*SOUND:*
*RECORD TRACK of MAS telling the story of*
*his younger brother Tats' whooping cough.*

MAS: (*recorded*) Just after we were taken off the train in Slocan City, uh, because many of the shacks were not built, they weren't ready, so they would put us in tents and it got cold enough at times the water in pails that were kept in the – inside the units – could be frozen. My youngest brother, Tats, who was about maybe two years old, or two and half years old, he was coughing, whooping, you know, I don't know, I guess it goes something like, uuuuh, you know, coughing in this tent. And that is one time when I was angry at the government, yeah, because I thought Tats, the youngest one, was gonna die there you know. Yeah, that's when I was really – really felt very hostile for the situation we were in.

> *TETSURO removes the tent from the mirror box and sets it on the upstage shelves, where it is illuminated by a narrow pin spot.*

# 8mm Intro

*After positioning the tent, TETSURO*
*faces the audience with the urgent energy*
*of someone who has a secret to share.*

Now what you are about to see marks the first time unauthorized footage of the internment has ever been screened publicly. You are among the very first people to ever see this.

> *PROJECTION:*
> *VIDEO of archival home-movie footage*
> *documenting the Lemon Creek internment camp.*

What is amazing about this footage, is that it *isn't* from the Canadian government's perspective, who referred to the Nikkei as "evacuees," implying that they were in need of being rescued from their middle-class lives. This is Lemon Creek, former cow pasture. In order to control the narrative, the Canadian government confiscated all personal cameras. Even children's toy cameras were taken away. Now, I want you to look here at the bottom of the screen. There's a man's shadow coming up.

(*to PROJECTIONIST*) Stop.

> *PROJECTION:*
> *The VIDEO freezes.*

I don't know anything about this man beyond the fact that he is reckless. I mean pulling the trigger on an 8mm movie camera in the middle of an internment camp? Why don't you go ahead and aim a starting pistol at a Mountie while you're at it? So reckless.

*PROJECTION:*
*VIDEO of archival home-movie footage resumes.*

So what did this rebel Nikkei so badly wish to document he was
willing to break the law? Whether it is in the big city or the middle
of nowhere, weddings are exciting. Something tells me getting
married wasn't *his* idea. Shotgun wedding, maybe? Look how well
dressed these Nikkei are. These are my people. I don't know where
this honeymoon getaway car thinks it's going; the other side of
camp maybe? Hopefully these newlyweds were able to fulfill other
nuptial traditions.

*PROJECTION:*
*VIDEO of grainy black-and-white film*
*footage of a fat baby fills the screen.*

Future sumo wrestler right there. Yokozuna!

*TETSURO punctuates this last remark with*
*the power move of an avid sports fan.*

# Lemon Creek: One of Twenty-Three

*TETSURO strides with vigour*
*downstage toward the audience.*

Does anyone here remember the address of your childhood home?

*TETSURO interacts briefly with the*
*audience, commenting on addresses*
*audience members volunteer.*

Mine is 13964 Talon Place. For my kids, it'll be 665 Royal Road
*(gestures toward the scale model).*

*TETSURO removes his blue suit jacket,*
*revealing a white button-up dress shirt with*
*brown leather detailing and vintage brown*
*leather suspenders. He folds the jacket into*
*one of the drawers in the upstage shelves.*

After the tents in Slocan City, the detainees got upgraded to those
shacks you just saw. When I asked Mas what his address was at
Lemon Creek, he did not hesitate. 64 Gilead.

*PROJECTION:*
*VIDEO of pan and scan of a blueprint*
*of the Lemon Creek internment camp.*
*Frame focuses on #64 Gilead.*

According to this blueprint Mas gave me, the Yamamotos lived
right here, 64 Gilead, right next to edge of the forest, which meant
there were sixty-four shacks on Gilead alone. Multiply that by
Cedar, Dogwood, Elm, Fir, Gilead, Holly, and Juniper, and you
have 266 shacks, each housing two families. In December of '42,
the population of Lemon Creek was nearly two thousand. Two

thousand souls is a lot of people, but Lemon Creek was just one camp. There were ten altogether –

> *PROJECTION:*
> *ANIMATED VIDEO of internment camps appearing on a map of British Columbia.*
>
> *TETSURO recites the names.*
>
> *SOUND:*
> *STEVE quietly hums under.*

Tashme,
Greenwood,
Slocan City,
Popoff,
Bay Farm,
Lemon Creek,
Sandon,
Kaslo,
New Denver, and
Rosebery.

Twenty if you count self-supporting settlements:
East Lillooet,
Bridge River,
Minto City,
McGillivray Falls,
Grand Forks,
Midway,
Blind Bay,
Taylor Lake,
Tappen, and
Christina Lake.

Almost sounds like a vacation spot, doesn't it?

Twenty-three if you count road-camp projects:
Hope to Princeton,
Revelstoke to Sicamous,
Blue River to Jasper along the Yellowhead.

Twenty-three places branded onto the memories of a generation of
Japanese Canadians. And as much as the injustice of it all galls me,
part of me can't help but admire the bureaucratic efficiency of it all.
Morality aside, I have to say, the Canadian government did a hell
of a job, moving more than twenty thousand Canadians with such
Teutonic efficiency. Then I realized, but of course! They wrote the
book. What did they call it? The Indian Act. They've been  practising
this for 150 years. Separating families, confiscating personal property,
policing movements, coercing elders into signing away birthrights on
documents they can't even read, confining entire communities onto
the worst land, legislating race-based laws, and then imprisoning
those who had the audacity to resist.

In 1942, all together twenty-one thousand Canadian citizens were
forcibly removed from their homes on the Pacific Coast to the
ghost towns I just mentioned. Now what do all these places have in
common? They're at least one hundred miles from the Pacific Coast,
because that's how much of a comfort zone British Columbians
needed in the event that the Imperial Japanese Navy came steaming
into English Bay to raise their flag over the Hotel Vancouver.

64 Gilead, Lemon Creek. If you try sending a postcard there today,
it'll be returned to sender because it is no longer there. There is
nothing left but a grassy field. No trace of the footpaths worn into
the ground by the two thousand adults who paced, the children
who ran, or the teenagers who sauntered.

*PROJECTION:*
*VIDEO of archival home-movie footage showing*
*everyday life in Lemon Creek internment camp.*

*SOUND:*
*RECORD TRACK of MAS describing*
*his teenage years at Lemon Creek.*

MAS: (*recorded*) In Lemon Creek, there was a couple of communal bathhouses, partitioned between men and women, and of course in those midteen years we were all interested in girls, and you know, the hormones were starting to course through our blood systems. Anyway, one of the girls that we knew, as soon as she went into the ladies' side, we'd dash into the men's side, hang ourselves from the rafters, and uh, like a couple of monkeys, we'd peek, "Oh yeah, look at that!" In those teenage years, that was the highlight.

> *TETSURO places a miniature log*
> *cabin in the mirror box and grabs the*
> *selfie stick and GoPro camera.*

For all the elaborate evils humankind can engineer to make adults despair, to make children sad, there has yet to be a scenario so depressing that young love cannot transcend it. Erect your walls, dig your trenches, but your obstacles are no match for adolescent hormones.

> *TETSURO executes another pan with the GoPro.*

*PROJECTION:*
*LIVE VIDEO of a log cabin repeated multiple*
*times in the walls of the mirror box.*

SOUND:
RECORD TRACK of MAS remembering
how he once held hands with Midge.

SOUND:
STEVE plays wistful music under.

MAS: (*recorded*) Her name was Midge Ayukawa. She was a bright girl. Always number one in class, but with Midge, it wasn't – obviously there was, uh, some physical attraction as well, but she wasn't a real gorgeous girl at that time. Pardon me, Midge. The closest we ever got was, we held hands as we walked. I remember carrying something, pots or whatever it was, after the dance. You know, we used to have to take stuff and she probably had her arms – so we only had one hand free and it was such a daring thing on my part to try to hold her hand. Yeah, I'm sure my hands were sweaty! But you know, physically, that was about as far as we – we were just kids at the time.

> STEVE *lifts the needle off the record,*
> *while TETSURO moves the mirror*
> *box to the upstage shelves.*

> TETSURO *looks expectantly up at*
> *the blank projection screen.*

~

# Yamamotos Go to Oyama

*The mood changes.*

*PROJECTION:*
*VIDEO of archival film footage showing*
*families leaving Lemon Creek by train,*
*young Japanese Canadians playing ice*
*hockey on a frozen lake, and an orchard.*

As quickly as Lemon Creek was built, when the war ended,
everyone was dispersed just like that. Would being released be
cause for celebration? Not if you can't move back into your old
home because a white family bought it for a song. Not if you
can't visit your old neighbourhood because you'll be arrested
for trespassing into the hundred-mile protected zone, which
remained in effect for years, even after the war was over. When
the war did end, the government gave Canadians of Japanese
descent two choices: (A) go "back" to Japan, which was a little
odd, considering most had never been there in the first place,
because they were born here. Or (B) move east of the Rockies.
The Yamamotos opted for (C) how about neither? The British
Columbia Security Commission was willing to turn a blind eye so
long as families promised to steer clear of Vancouver, and if they
could find a way to support themselves somehow. Somewhere
in the Okanagan, in a place called Oyama, an orchard needed
caretakers. So the Yamamotos, a once proud fishermen clan, now
picked apples. Once late at night when Mas was a teenager, his
mother called him to the kitchen table.

*PROJECTION:*
*VIDEO of an older Japanese woman in*
*silhouette, sitting at table. A young MAS*
*in silhouette sits down across from her.*

*SOUND:*
*RECORD TRACK of MAS describing his teenage*
*years working in the orchards at Oyama.*

MAS: (*recorded*) Must have been about eighteen. One
night, my mother took me aside, I guess she must have
asked me to sit down and chat. We were sitting at a table
like this, and it was dusk, it was quite dark, and I guess
my brothers and sisters were in bed, and that's when she
gave me a talk. What she said was, I needed to be strong,
because I was needed to put bread and butter on the table.
I put my head down on my arms like this, you know, and I
might have cried a bit. Yeah. It's almost as though she was
telling me, "Say goodbye to your youth."

*PROJECTION:*
*VIDEO of young MAS and his mother in*
*silhouette cross-fades, leaving the shape of*
*present-day MAS sitting at the table alone.*

*Standing upstage right, TETSURO watches*
*the screen with a sense of wonder.*

≈

# Movie of Our Lives

*Spotlight downstage centre. TETSURO*
*steps into the spotlight.*

In the movie of our lives, we perform for an audience of one.
For some, that is an all-seeing God. But for others, we choose
our director to be someone whose approval we desire. We try to
become the kind of person they would find worth watching. Even
after they leave us, we continue to hold vigil, as if our faithful
posture might be rewarded with their return.

> *PROJECTION:*
> *VIDEO of STILL IMAGES of MAS and*
> *Midge. Mas' photo shows his handwritten*
> *signature in the top-left corner. He signed*
> *his photos before sending them to Midge.*
>
> *SOUND:*
> *RECORD TRACK of MAS remembering*
> *the dark days after the war.*

MAS: (*recorded*) We kept in touch. She used to send me, you
know, letters – pink envelope and that sort of thing. She said she
was going to attend McMaster University, and here I was working
in an orchard, you know, picking apples, and irrigating, pruning
during the winter, and just feeling that there was absolutely no
hope, no future, but I remember taking a twenty-two rifle, which
I borrowed. There was a cat that was really bugging me. Yeah,
maybe I should put an end to that cat's life, and at the same time I
thought to myself, why not shoot myself? I picture those years in
the Okanagan as being in a tunnel, in a deep tunnel, with no hope,
everything is dark, and if I can only find a little pinhole of light.

*TETSURO lifts the needle off the*
*record on the turntable.*

When we become old enough to look back upon our lives, it's easy to recognize that lowest point, the nadir. That moment when we don't know if we can survive, but we do. We always find a reason to keep on going, until we don't.

> *PROJECTION:*
> *VIDEO of archival home-movie footage of a*
> *family of Japanese Canadian kids, followed by*
> *STILL IMAGES alternating between images of*
> *a young MAS and images of a young Midge.*
>
> *TETSURO places the needle on the vinyl record.*
>
> *SOUND:*
> *RECORD TRACK of MAS comparing his*
> *life after the war with that of Midge.*

MAS: (*recorded*) Well, at that time, I guess I was about eighteen, nineteen. I still had brothers and sisters. Somebody had to provide for them. Yeah, and so Midge she went on and got her master's degree. I could see she was getting ahead in life and I just wasn't, that I would be irrigating orchards and picking apples for the rest of my life. I guess in my head I was thinking at that time that I'm not good enough for her, really, yeah. So I wrote a Dear Jane letter, I guess, that there was no future in our relationship. I didn't have any hope at that time of bettering myself with just a grade nine high school education, whereas she was going on to her – and that's the last I was in touch with her.

> *TETSURO remains upstage, held under the spell*
> *of Mas' story and the photos that have now faded.*

Mas in a snowy Oyama orchard, 1952. *George Metcalf Archival Collection, Canadian War Museum, CWM 20150279-002P84.*

Midge awarded Honours Chemistry (BSc), McMaster University, May 1952.
*George Metcalf Archival Collection, Canadian War Museum, CWM 20150279-002-57.*

## UFO Thought Experiment

*As if waking from a dream, TETSURO*
*strides downstage centre and addresses*
*both STEVE and the audience.*

You are walking alone at night, and you are visited by a UFO.
And you are given the following offer: Come with us, and you
will see things for which there are no words in any of your
languages, but we're leaving right now. No time for goodbyes. No
time for explanations. Would you go? Think about it. You'd be
one of those people who mysteriously vanish one day and end
up as a photo on a missing-persons poster. Me, I think I'd go.
Even though it's a terrible thing to say, because I have a young
family. But a part of me is still a kid, and I wanna see. Sure my
kids would be sad, but as the earth became smaller, I would
make a vow. I would do my utmost to make it known to them
that I have not forgotten them. And I realize this is to enter the
realm of the esoteric, but I have to believe there must be a way
to let someone know that you still think about them. Because it
shouldn't matter if it's halfway around the world, or across the
universe, I believe when you hold someone so closely in your
thoughts, part of them must feel that energy coming their way,
the way the mothers of POWs during World War II, long after
their governments declared their loved ones dead, deep down
they had an inkling that their child was still alive. Just the most
quiet form of knowledge, without words, but unwavering.

*TETSURO moves to the lazy Susan and places the*
*GoPro with selfie stick on the edge. Lights shift.*

PROJECTION:
*LIVE VIDEO of Tetsuro's fingers walking across the lazy Susan and stopping halfway across.*

*STEVE begins singing "Idumea," a Methodist shape note hymn.*

PROJECTION:
*LIVE VIDEO of Tetsuro's fingers levitating for a moment, before being drawn upwards out of the frame.*

*Then, for a moment, Tetsuro's spread fingers glow, warmly backlit from a pin spot above; then they swoop through the top of the frame, suggesting a UFO flying past.*

*Spotlight on TETSURO as he stands facing the audience as STEVE continues singing. They sing the last line together.*

STEVE and TETSURO: "Into a world unknown."

*A moment of silence as the afterglow of the imagery and the echo of the singing fades.*

# Heart's Compass

*Lights shift as TETSURO advances*
*toward the audience.*

My friend Phil once asked me for romantic advice. He said, "My friend is going up north for work. I'm not sure when I'll see her again, so I want to give her something to let her know how I feel." We went into a thrift shop, and we're looking at stuff in the glass display case. "This, buy her this old toy compass. Place it in her hand and say, 'When things get hard for you up there, and you are feeling all alone, take this out and find true north, and know I am standing directly behind you, holding you in my thoughts.'"

*TETSURO holds out an imaginary*
*compass and extends his hand to an*
*audience member in the balcony.*

# The Cold War

*SOUND:*
*STEVE plays some fifties-style guitar riffs.*

*The rhythm enters Tetsuro's body*
*through his foot and travels up his leg,*
*until it takes over his whole body.*

The year is 1955, and even though I was not yet born, some of the things I have mixed feelings about were just being introduced. The very first McDonalds opened its doors. 1955 was the year the beloved bottle of Coke began being replaced by red aluminum cans. *The Mickey Mouse Club* debuted on TV and would eventually gift us with Britney Spears, Justin Timberlake, and "Hey, Girl" Ryan Gosling. Sony began selling its first transistor radios in Japan, and Rosa Parks was arrested for refusing to give up her seat to a white passenger in Montgomery, Alabama. But what was happening in Canada? A lot, actually.

*TETSURO moves upstage right.*

*PROJECTION:*
*VIDEO of excerpts from the archival*
*film* The DEW Line Story *(1958)*
*by AT&T–Western Electric.*

1950s FILM NARRATOR: The Arctic: desolate, savage, remote ... yet this roof of the world holds a stark menace to our country, to our very existence ... what was once the impassable Arctic now provides the quickest routes for attack from a wide sector of Europe and Asia. Beset by the nightmare of this threat ... the nation's leaders decided on a tremendous undertaking. This was to build, with the co-operation of Canada, a radar early warning line north of the Arctic Circle. Starting at the northernmost tip of Alaska, it would stretch three thousand miles across the continent to Baffin Island opposite Greenland. "Distant Early Warning Line" they named it. "DEW Line" it became.

*TETSURO moves downstage centre.*

As a Nikkei without a high school diploma, Mas' employment options were limited. So he journeyed north to the top of the world, where he went from being public enemy number one to a trusted ally in the fight against a new enemy, communism. His title? Industrial first aid attendant for the largest military industrial project ever undertaken, the DEW Line. At the age of twenty-eight, Mas opens his very first bank account.

*STEVE hands TETSURO the*
*transparent vinyl record.*

For the first time in his life, the money he's making is going into his *own* pocket and not the mouths of his siblings. 1955 would be the most important year of Mas' life, the axis upon which his world turns from night to day.

*TETSURO holds up the record and*
*flips from the A side to the B side. He*
*places the record on the turntable.*

*SOUND:*
*STEVE plays haunting chords*
*suggesting music of the spheres.*

*Stage left, a pale white light casts*
*long Arctic shadows.*

*Staring at the light, TETSURO crosses*
*slowly to centre stage as if in a trance. He*
*stands in front of the projection screen.*

SOUND:
*RECORD TRACK of MAS relating*
*his first impressions of the Arctic.*

MAS: (*recorded*) I recall how flat it was. Quite, I guess, I don't know whether I'd use the word "beautiful" or not, but it was – the Arctic in its own way can be quite, uh, pretty. Summertime was daylight like this twenty-four hours a day, it's unreal, you know. Well the sun just circles, basically, you know, down over your head, around. Yeah. Not in a perfect circle but, you know, up high and then down close to the horizon and up again.

*Lights go down and the stage is in darkness.*

PROJECTION:
*VIDEO of present-day MAS in silhouette as if he*
*were a shadow cast from TETSURO, who stands*
*downstage centre, looking out at the horizon as*
*the light and sound transform with the dawn.*

SOUND:
*RECORD TRACK of MAS describing*
*the first sunrise at the end of winter.*

MAS: (*recorded*) You hadn't seen the sun – a couple of months of darkness. It got quite bright on the horizon, kind of an orangey colour I guess, orange-red, yeah, but to actually see that fiery – that piece of fire out there and disappear, then suddenly you felt alive again. Yeah, it was a – almost like a spiritual experience! Because if you go through a couple of months or more, essentially in complete darkness, it's nice to see that sun, you feel suddenly alive again. Like life is returning somehow.

> *TETSURO moves to the turntable*
> *to scratch the last phrase.*

MAS: (*recorded*) Like life is returning somehow. Like life is returning somehow.

> *TETSURO lifts the needle.*

Joan Ishikawa at the Aquatic Building in Penticton, 1948. *Marie Ishikawa (sister).*

# Hierarchy of Love

*As if remember something, TETSURO steps away*
*from the turntable and strides toward the audience.*

TETSURO: In the hierarchy of love, we have the soulmate and the one-night stand, but can't someone be a soulmate for just one night? Steve?

STEVE: Oh yeah, definitely.

TETSURO: Sometimes, it takes a fling to launch ourselves toward eternity.

> *Lights go down. TETSURO stands aside stage left.*

> *SOUND:*
> *STEVE plays dancehall music on the keyboard,*
> *building under to set the era – date night in 1955!*

> *SOUND:*
> *RECORD TRACK of MAS and*
> *his first blind date with Joan.*

MAS: (*recorded*) I was about twenty-eight or so, twenty-nine. Remember I was up in the Arctic for a whole year and there was nobody except a few Eskimos. I didn't even see any ladies up there, and a friend of mine asked me one time, do you want to go on a blind date? And so I said, yeah, I've been out of circulation for a while. Was introduced to Joan, and obviously she was the most beautiful girl I had ever seen for a whole year. And I was just carried away, just a physical attraction because she was beautiful. I don't know what she saw in me.

PROJECTION:
STILL IMAGE of JOAN, circa 1950s,
wearing a bathing suit, looking very much
like an Alberto Vargas pin-up girl.

SOUND:
STEVE continues to play dancehall music under.

So the permafrost of Mas' arctic celibacy thawed beneath this new heavenly body. Joan Ishikawa and Mas Yamamoto were soon married. Mas' job had him on-site at the Bridge River Project, a hydroelectric dam built to meet the insatiable postwar appetite for energy.

*TETSURO goes to the lazy Susan, places a miniature double bed on the outside edge, close to the GoPro camera, at waist height. He begins a fingerplay with two fingers bouncing on the double bed and then running and running in front of the camera to get back to bouncing on the bed again, which reappears in the frame repeatedly.*

PROJECTION:
*LIVE VIDEO of fingerplay of double-bed steeplechase.*

SOUND:
*RECORD TRACK of MAS recollecting his early years of married life when he worked away from home.*

MAS: (*recorded*) We decided, okay, if I'm going to go to – if I want to continue, go to university, then we'll have to make some sacrifices, and one was for her to – even after we got married she stayed at home in Vancouver. Just being newly married, you know, I remember as soon as Friday, five o'clock or so when my shift

ended. God, you know, I used to drive like mad, and it used to –
at that time it used to take me six hours to drive, and I'd spend all
day Saturday and Sunday with her. Obviously we spent some time
in bed. We'd get up, and I remember having lunch or breakfast,
I've forgotten. She had another unmarried – at that time Bill, her
brother – somehow she had to mention, "Hey Bill, we broke the
bed." And Bill was so embarrassed, he didn't know what to do!

> TETSURO *returns the miniature double bed*
> *to one of the drawers in the upstage shelves.*
>
> SOUND:
> STEVE *plays progressively climbing chords*
> *on the keyboard, suggesting the scales of*
> *a relentlessly diligent piano student.*

Twenty lessons. That's how many booklets you must complete
in order to be awarded "senior matriculation," a grade thirteen
graduation certificate. Each lesson takes two weeks to complete,
but Mas isn't walking through them. He's running. His pen pal
instructor admonishes him to "slow down!" He can't grade the
lessons as fast as Mas is completing them. Mas writes back.

> SOUND:
> AUDIO CLIP *of* MAS *recalling*
> *his drive to get an education.*
>
> MAS: (*recorded*) I just don't have the time to – I am a
> mature student trying to catch up [*laughs*].
>
> PROJECTION:
> VIDEO *of* STILL IMAGES *showing* MAS
> *at his various jobs throughout the years.*

Mas is trying to outrun his blue-collar past, away from carrying
lumber at the sawmill in Revelstoke, away from pounding spikes
on the train tracks in Glacier, away from picking apples in the

orchard in Oyama, away from being a psychiatric male nurse at
Essondale in Coquitlam, away from being an industrial first aid
attendant in the Arctic and on the Bridge River dam project. He
crosses the finish line in record time. High school diploma in hand,
he enrols in the University of British Columbia, at the tender age
of thirty-two, into the Faculty of Pharmacy. Why pharmacy?

> SOUND:
> Piano scales continue to climb.

> SOUND:
> AUDIO CLIP of MAS explaining his
> reasons to get a professional degree.

MAS: (recorded) Because I could put on a nice white coat
and I would not have to work in the rain.

> SOUND:
> STEVE transitions on the keyboard into Pomp
> and Circumstance March in D Major, Op. 39,
> No. 1, by English composer Edward Elgar (1901).

> TETSURO pulls a red plastic View-Master
> from one of the drawers in the upstage shelves
> and looks through the toy stereoscope. Each
> time TETSURO pulls the trigger, a new set
> of identical images appears onscreen.

Leaving the muddied work boots of his past out in the hallway,
Mas enters the university lecture hall where the rest of the students
are about half his age, but Mas earns top marks. Invigorated
by conjugal bliss, energized by marital happiness, he gets his
bachelor's of science in 1962, he gets his master's in pharmacology
in 1964, and in 1966 at the age of thirty-nine, he gets his PhD.
That's three university degrees in just seven years. His doctoral
thesis? "Studies on heart muscle lipases and cyclic nucleotide

phosphodiesterase" – in plain English, Mas was asking, what is the energy source of the heart?

> *PROJECTION:*
> *VIDEO of STILL IMAGES illustrates the passage*
> *of time: Mas' graduation certificates, journal*
> *publications, and family photos of his children.*

Mas becomes a research scientist for the government and publishes in the top journals of his field. These are the happiest years of his life, because he's not just fruitful as a scholar, but as a father. His wife, Joan, gives him a daughter named Naomi, another daughter named Donna, and a son named Brian.

> *PROJECTION:*
> *VIDEO closes on STILL IMAGE of Joan,*
> *Donna, Naomi, and Brian, 1967.*

> *Lights down.*

> *TETSURO returns the View-Master*
> *to a drawer in the upstage shelves.*

# Seahorse

*Lights up. TETSURO goes to the upstage shelves, retrieves a box of photos, moves to the lazy Susan, and begins to sort through them. STEVE joins him.*

Funny how the palette of our own age is always invisible to us. Its change is so slow, it's imperceptible, like the drift of continents making us forget that the past took place in colour, and it's only the hindsight of decades that allows us to recognize the now unmistakable orange cast of seventies Kodak film. We remember the eighties in cool, saturated tones courtesy of Fujifilm. White borders give way to full bleed, corners become rounded, time-stamps burn like brands from the O.K. Corral. Inseparable from our memories is the photographic paper they were printed on. Do we remember memories, or do recollect photographs?

*TETSURO puts the photos back into the lidded box and returns the box to the upstage shelves.*

I have a memory I used to question because there is no related photograph to prove it ever happened. So this first part I will admit is pure speculation, but I must have been sitting with my father on the floating dock in the middle of the lake at Camp Green Bay, and I suppose I suggested to him, "Hey, Dad, when you swim ashore, how about I ride on your back?" And this is where my mental snapshot comes into focus. I'm riding my dad like a seahorse, whooping it up, and I can see my mom standing on the shore, frowning at us, which was not her usual expression. Years later I asked my mom if she shared my memory, or was this something I was just imagining?

> TETSURO *responds LIVE to*
> *RECORDED AUDIO.*
>
> *SOUND:*
> *AUDIO of Tetsuro's MOM, Yoshiko.*

MOM: (*recorded*) No, I do remember.

TETSURO: (*live*) Why did you look so worried?

MOM: (*recorded*) I wasn't sure if your father could make it all the way back to shore.

TETSURO: (*live*) Well, if Dad was in trouble, why didn't he just call out for help?

MOM: (*recorded*) And call attention to himself? I think he would sooner drown.

TETSURO: (*live*) So how did you know Dad was in trouble?

MOM: (*recorded*) Well, because he was ... smiling.

> *PROJECTION:*
> *VIDEO STILL of the underside of*
> *Akira's nose, circa the late seventies. This*
> *accidental snapshot dissolves into a recent*
> *photograph of Mr. and Mrs. Shigematsu*
> *taken outdoors about forty years later.*

This is my father's own attempt at photography. Unlike Mas, and myself, my dad never developed an affinity for the camera. Toward the end of my father's life, it fell to me to act as his medical advocate. I accompanied him on all his visits to all the medical specialists, in order to help my mother make decisions about my father's end-of-life care. My father once confided to his geriatric psychiatrist (*as AKIRA*), "Every day I wake up disappointed I am still alive." (*as TETSURO*) To which the good doctor replied –

STEVE: (*as DOCTOR*) Mr. Shigematsu, if you no longer wish to live, what is preventing you from ending it?

TETSURO: (*as AKIRA*) The sooner I die, the longer I will have to wait for my wife in the hereafter.

*TETSURO looks up thoughtfully. Lights shift.*

~

# Reset Button

*TETSURO snaps out of his reverie.*

Now in his fifties, Mas had lived several lifetimes already, but that doesn't mean he was immune from having a midlife crisis. Mas realized, as good a scientist as he was, born to it, he would never overcome the "ten-year Lemon Creek handicap" to reach the front of the pack.

> *SOUND:*
> *RECORD TRACK of MAS telling how*
> *he first learned about the one-hour film-*
> *processing business from one of his kids.*

MAS: (*recorded*) Naomi one summer – a university student – was working at a small business – I think it was downtown somewhere – and she'd come home and she talked about this machine that converted, you know, the film into negatives and pictures in one hour! And so I would ask her, how many customers, how much money does this company make? Much to her credit, lips were sealed tight, yup, she wouldn't tell me. That was all loyalty, I mean, after all, she was working for somebody else, not for me. So I remember going to this – sitting in front of the windows – sitting there and watching and, you know, the pictures coming down, and I thought, geez, looks like this is a real good business, so I checked into it. At that time there was an outfit called Japan Camera.

So one day, Mas comes home and says to Joan, "Remember all those years of sacrifice for me to get a PhD, living apart when we were newlyweds, raising the kids pretty much all on your own? Well you can forget about all of that. I'm done with being a scientist."

> SOUND:
> AUDIO CLIP of the opening notes
> of Van Halen's "Jump."

> TETSURO struts and prances about
> the stage like a hair metal rock star.

The year is 1980, and Mas is at the height of his powers. He has all the virile swagger of a young Humphrey Bogart in *Two Against the World*, and all the worldly wisdom of old Bogie in *Casablanca*. So while others his age are thinking about retirement, at the age of fifty-three, Mas is ready to start over – again!

> Lights shift as TETSURO walks upstage right.

~

## Mas Tests Joan

*TETSURO stands behind the scale*
*model of 665 Royal Road.*

*PROJECTION:*
*VIDEO of STILL IMAGES of MAS and family*
*working in the Japan Camera shop, circa the 1980s.*

*SOUND:*
*RECORD TRACK of MAS talking about running*
*his own one-hour film-processing business.*

MAS: (*recorded*) At the beginning, when we were just
starting, with only one store in Capilano Mall – just a teeny
four-hundred-square-foot store, but it was tremendously
successful. I mean we were competing with all the other
one-hour photo stores across Canada, and we were number
one in sales. I mean it was just a gold mine! But we worked
hard, both working late, every day, seven days a week –
then, when we started the store, because I guess we were
kind of worried that we had to – we had no option but to
succeed. To fail would have been just disastrous, you know,
because I mortgaged the house and everything.

*TETSURO stares at the projection screen*
*as the last photo of MAS working in his*
*Japan Camera shop fades from view.*

≈

## Mom's Diary

*TETSURO stands above the scale model of
665 Royal Road holding the GoPro camera
with the selfie stick and a small flashlight. The
tiny microphone is still on the dining room
table. TETSURO puts it away and sets out an
equally small Bible, notebook, and chair.*

*PROJECTION:
LIVE VIDEO of the GoPro camera wandering
over the miniature dining room table until it
comes to rest on Tetsuro's Mom's red diary.*

My little family lives together with my mom now, and every night
before she goes to sleep, she writes in her diary right here at this
kitchen table. Sometimes I'll ask her to read me what happened
one year ago today, the last time our planet was in this position in
its orbit around the sun. It's easy for her, because that particular
entry will be on the exact same page. My mom has been keeping
journals her whole life. And if she goes back far enough, there is an
entry where I do not exist.

I once asked my mom to read me next year's entry. She smiled and
said, "It hasn't been written yet." Now I'm not one to share Bible
verses with my mom – that'd be like giving a stock tip to Warren
Buffet – but there is a verse I think about as I watch her writing in her
diary: Psalm 139, verse 16. "For all your days are written in my book."
The Bible and science don't always agree, but according to theoretical
physics, all your days may have already happened – all of them.

*TETSURO turns off his flashlight and
removes the GoPro camera from the
scale model of 665 Royal Road.*

## Multiple Exposure

*Lights shift.*

Imagine bringing in a roll of film, ready to be developed, and when you go to pick it up an hour later, all you get back is a thin envelope containing just one photograph? Sometimes, back in the day when you loaded a roll of film into your camera, if the sprockets didn't catch the film leader properly, every time you pulled the transport lever, the film itself wouldn't actually advance, and what you would end up with was all your moments exposed onto a single frame. The cool thing was, if you didn't toss this photograph, if you looked closely, you could still see everything.

> *PROJECTION:*
> *VIDEO of a multiple exposure of photos*
> *from every stage of Mas' life.*
>
> *SOUND:*
> *STEVE begins layering in every musical*
> *theme within the show thus far, one on*
> *top of another, creating an increasingly*
> *trippy, harmonic cacophony.*

What you are looking at may be a reflection of the true nature of existence. Some believe that time is an illusion of human perception that enables us to parse through reality moment by moment, because that's all our primate brains can handle as we cling to this rock spinning around a ball of fire.

> *TETSURO looks out into space as if he*
> *is witnessing a cosmic phenomenon.*

≈

## Gentle Death

*TETSURO peers down into the scale
model of the house. It jogs a memory.*

One night, I sat next to my father watching him sleep. I was
thinking about a conversation we had earlier that day. I had asked
him how he had been feeling lately. He said he was physically and
emotionally exhausted. "Why emotionally?"

TETSURO: (*as AKIRA*) I'm ready to leave this planet.

TETSURO: Why would you say that?

TETSURO: (*as AKIRA*) Because there are no positive
contributions I can make. I spend all my days in bed.

TETSURO: What about your grandchildren? Aren't they
worth sticking around for?

I thought this reasoning had gotten through to him, because he
took a really long time to respond. Turns out, he had fallen asleep.
I could hear the wind chimes outside. Death was in the room that
day. Not the red death of terror, long in claw and fang, just soft,
gentle death.

*Lights shift.*

≈

# Reunion

*TETSURO crosses to the turntable stage left.*

*SOUND:*
*RECORD TRACK of MAS talking about meeting*
*Midge again for the first time in many years.*

MAS: (*recorded*) I had completed my years as a scientist, switched over to the business world, and when I opened up another store, an outlet in Victoria, who should come into the store but Midge?

*SOUND:*
*STEVE returns to playing 1950s*
*dancehall music on the keyboard.*

Imagine seeing your first love after a whole lifetime has passed. Mas and Midge recognized each other instantly. Despite everything that time does to us, what a gift to be recognized for who you were and seen for who you are.

*TETSURO drops the needle on the record.*

*SOUND:*
*RECORD TRACK of MAS recalling the flowers*
*he sent to Midge after he had found her again.*

MAS: (*recorded*) Midge, during that time, she was herself studying for her PhD. Of course I was finished my PhD a long time ago. I thought, oh wow, that's great. Went to florist, and I said, "Look, here's some money, send all these flowers to her." I phoned her to congratulate her, and she couldn't, she said she was overwhelmed by the amount of flowers that were delivered. I said I didn't know.

*PROJECTION:*
*VIDEO of black-and-white 8mm film footage of*
*cherry trees at Lemon Creek becomes gradually*
*colourized. Cross-fade into a close-up of delicate*
*cherry blossoms in full colour and full bloom.*

*SOUND:*
*RECORD TRACK of MAS relating the*
*story of seeing Midge again in later life.*

MAS: (*recorded*) The last time I saw her – I did phone
Midge, and she was invited to Naomi's speech, I guess, and
a whole bunch of us sat in the gallery.

*PROJECTION:*
*VIDEO of North Vancouver–Lonsdale (Liberal)*
*MLA, then Minister of Advanced Education,*
*Naomi Yamamoto's ministerial speech in the 39th*
*Parliament of the B.C. Legislature on May 7,*
*2012, proposing a provincial government apology*
*for Japanese Canadian internment during World*
*War II, from* Hansard 37.2: 11578–11580.

NAOMI: (*recorded*) Thank you, Mr. Speaker. In the
Canada of today we are blessed to live in an open,
inclusive, and multicultural society. In 1941 this was not
the case for my father, Mas, a Canadian citizen. While
attending Point Grey Junior Secondary at the age of
fourteen, he loved school and he loved being a cadet. But
one day in December of that year Mas was called to the
principal's office, along with some of his Japanese Canadian
school buddies who were cadets as well.

...

Because they were no longer permitted to participate in cadets. My dad was stunned when the principal said: "We are at war with your people, and precautions must be taken." My dad suddenly realized that the word "we" did not include him and that "your people" meant the Japanese. He thought to himself: "The Japanese aren't our people. Our people are Canadians."

They left the principal's office numb. His mother had just sent him to school to buy war stamps to support Canada's war efforts.

...

And on March 24, 1942, my dad, his brothers and sisters, and their mother – my grandmother – had just twenty-four hours to pack up their belongings before being relocated.

...

The Canadian government assured the Japanese Canadians that their homes, fishing boats, and other assets would be returned upon their release. Instead, they were sold off at auction for cents on the dollar.

Unlike prisoners of war, who are protected by the Geneva Convention, Japanese Canadians had to pay for their own internment in this way.

...

The war ended in 1945, and the abuses continued. Canadians of Japanese descent were ordered to move east of the Rockies or be shipped to war-torn Japan.

...

It wasn't until 1949 [that] Japanese Canadians were legally permitted to return to B.C.'s west coast.

My dad was twenty-two in 1949, without a high school education, but the year is significant. In 1949 Canadians of Japanese descent gained their right to vote. And sixty years later, in 2009, I was honoured to become the first Canadian of Japanese descent to be elected to B.C.'s Legislative Assembly.

Now, this House has heard me tell the story of the barriers that my dad overcame to complete his high school education by correspondence. He eventually earned a PhD in pharmacology at UBC about twenty years after the end of the war. He did that working full-time and raising kids. He's in the House today at a different time in our history.

This is a story of one small family. The scope and breadth of what was done to so many Canadians by virtue of their ethnicity ...

...

And not a single Japanese Canadian was ever charged with an act of disloyalty.

Despite these injustices, hardships, and acts of discrimination, most of the interned chose not to be bitter. Instead they rolled up their sleeves and rebuilt their lives and their communities once they were allowed to return home. The painful details of these times were generally not shared with their children until many years later because there was too much work to be done.

...

This year marks the seventieth anniversary of the internment, and so it is fitting for us to take time to reflect on this moment in our province's history and commit to ensuring that nothing like this ever happens again. I would urge both sides of the House to support this motion, a formal apology to the Japanese Canadian community, as a reaffirmation of our commitment to be a welcoming society free of discrimination in any form. There are people in this gallery today who deserve this. Thank you. [*applause*]

*The motion carried unanimously.*

When Mas and Midge said goodbye to each other for the very last time in Lemon Creek at the end of the war, Midge must have seemed like the kind of person voted Most Likely to Go Far – far away, like a comet. So is it any wonder that Mas would spend the rest of his life becoming a kind of astronaut always reaching for the stars? But for all his calculations, who could have predicted their orbits would intersect half a century later?

> *STEVE lowers the needle as TETSURO walks over to the turntable and stands behind it.*

> *SOUND:*
> *RECORD TRACK of MAS as he remembers seeing Midge at a party following Naomi Yamamoto's ministerial speech in the B.C. Legislature.*

MAS: (*recorded*) After the apology speech was made, we did get together in Naomi's office. By then I guess I had regained some of the self-confidence that I had lost from the days in the Okanagan. My gosh, what are you talking about? Almost fifty years. And yeah, that's when Midge and I did get a chance to a chat a little bit, but there were so many people milling around. Damn it, you know, I wish I had taken time off, or taken a bit of time, and, and discussed some of these things, her thoughts, how she felt at that time, but I was kind of concerned because she – just probably had some kind of physical ailment.

I can't remember how long after that, I heard or read that she had passed away, and I've – I asked around if she was buried in Victoria or whether she was, uh, buried out east somewhere with her family, but I never did find out, no. But there is one thing I did wanna do, was to – kind of chokes me up a bit when I talk about it – but I did want to find her, to leave a flower or something, you know, on her grave. I wouldn't even utter any words. I think it would be just inside me.

*TETSURO lifts the needle off the record.*

## Undermining Your Immaculate Conceptions

*TETSURO looks up from the turntable*
*and turns toward the audience.*

*PROJECTION:*
*VIDEO of STILL IMAGES of Midge, then*
*Joan. Then Midge fades out, leaving only Joan.*

Midge and Joan. Joan and Midge. Who would you rather be? The one you can't forget, or the one you can't live without? For me, the hardest part in hearing Mas' story was putting myself in his kids' shoes. If I learned my dad had carried a torch, I wouldn't like it. We can accept complexity and nuance in our own hearts, but when it comes to our parents, it's hard to hear that, before Mom and Dad first met, there was another. This isn't the fairy tale they read to us.

*TETSURO lingers downstage centre for a moment,*
*before returning to the scale model of the house.*

~

# Death of Joan

*TETSURO and STEVE move the
plinth supporting the scale model of
665 Royal Road downstage.*

*SOUND:
AUDIO CLIP of MAS remembering the
last minutes of his wife Joan's life.*

MAS: (*recorded*) I thought I was very unemotional when
it comes to people, you know, passing, dying. I knew
that Joan, for example, was going to die, and she had lost
consciousness, and uh, it was just a matter of watching her
take a last breath. After she passed away, I was very calm. I
notified the nurse, but I do remember Joan's younger sister
coming to visit, and that's when I broke down. It was just an
involuntary thing. The stoicism I showed at the time, or for
years, really was a front.

*TETSURO and STEVE ready the scale
model of the house for one last projection.*

# Death of Akira

*TETSURO looks up from the house*
*to the projection screen.*

*PROJECTION:*
*LIVE VIDEO of the GoPro camera's birds-eye-*
*view of the scale-model house, showing Akira's*
*room dominated by the miniature hospital bed.*

*STEVE shines an iPhone flashlight*
*through the glass French doors, simulating*
*the slanting rays of a setting sun.*

My father died right here in the corner of this room. He was unconscious, and I was practically lying across him, watching his chest move, like a surfer watching for ocean swells. There would be nothing, and I'd think, is that it? Then all of a sudden, he'd inhale, like an afterthought. These abrupt inhalations became further and further apart, until he stopped.

*STEVE removes the iPhone flashlight,*
*while TETSURO returns the GoPro*
*camera to the dining room in its first*
*position at the beginning of the show.*

Background: the room where my father died. Foreground: the room where I interviewed Mas. *Tetsuro Shigematsu.*

## Epilogue

*TETSURO walks toward centre stage*
*and gestures toward the screen.*

Everything that happened in this room was driven by a question:
How does one live?

> *PROJECTION:*
> *LIVE VIDEO of GoPro camera on the scale-*
> *model house. The audience sees the kitchen wall,*
> *like the first interior shot of the model house*
> *looking at Mas' chair. But this time, the middle*
> *wall magically becomes transparent, making*
> *the contents of both rooms visible. Now, the*
> *hospital bed and IV pole in the back bedroom,*
> *as well as the original dining room setup with*
> *the microphone are both visible in the frame.*

What happened in this room left me wondering, what is a
good death? Although they may sound like different questions,
how to live, how to die, I think the answers might be the same:
surrounded by loved ones and free of regret. But what does that
even mean, "to live without regret"? Maybe it means less of this –

> *SOUND:*
> *AUDIO CLIP of MAS as he recalls*
> *meeting Midge in later life.*

MAS: (*recorded*) Damn it, you know, I wish I had taken
time off, or taken a bit of time and, and discussed some of
these things, her thoughts. How she felt at that time.

And more of this –

*SOUND:*
*AUDIO CLIP of MAS as he recalls*
*making a move on young Midge.*

MAS: (*recorded*) And it was such a daring thing on my part to try to hold her hand. Yeah, I'm sure my hands were sweaty! [*laughing*]

> *TETSURO removes the contents of his father's*
> *room: the miniature hospital bed and the IV pole.*

A month and a half after my father died, I began my conversations with Mas.

> *TETSURO moves downstage left to the*
> *turntable, where STEVE hands over the*
> *vinyl record. TETSURO returns to centre*
> *stage and speaks while holding the record.*

This record of my friend's voice is very precious to me. When I arranged to have it pressed, I had this fantasy of his grandchildren, or even his great-grandchildren, sitting down with a record player and listening to it one day, somewhere, in the future. But I realize chances are it's more likely to get lost or end up in some cosmic garage sale.

> *TETSURO holds up the transparent*
> *vinyl record one last time.*

NASA had similar concerns for Voyager. What if the Golden Record collided with an asteroid or ended up as target practice for Klingons?

> *TETSURO places the record face out on*
> *a small easel in the final open space left on*
> *the upstage shelves, the very centre.*

So they built not one spacecraft, but two.

*TETSURO returns to the scale-model
house and begins to disassemble it, placing
each piece in the cupboards behind him.*

Even as we speak, Voyager 1 is headed for Camelopardalis.
Voyager 2 is headed for Andromeda. Genius. In like manner,
instead of pressing one record, I pressed twenty. Stupid. I only now
realize I don't have twenty trusted guardians. All I have is you.

*SOUND:
STEVE plays haunting cosmic chords
on his vintage electric jazz guitar.*

This record of Mas' voice is now etched in your memory. Each
one of you is a vessel, and in just a few minutes, you'll be
headed to all points. I wish I could see what you will see, those
close encounters for which there are no words in any of your
languages. I will leave you with a Norwegian proverb: "Heroism
consists in hanging on one minute longer, just one minute." To
me, that one minute of earth time is equivalent to a one-second
pulse from a small rocket thruster.

*TETSURO has finished disassembling the
house. All that is left on the plinth is the
wooden floor and the dining room set.*

You see, if it takes a huge rocket to lift a Volkswagen off the
planet, once you're in the vacuum of space, all it takes is a very
small rocket to make fine adjustments. These small rockets aren't
powerful enough to change your course 180 degrees, but given
enough distance, even the smallest adjustment in attitude can alter
your trajectory from one world to another.

*TETSURO rotates the plinth so the dining
room table comes closer to the audience.*

*SOUND:*
*STEVE plays one last chord: melancholic*
*but humming with energy.*

*Lights fade to black. All that remains illuminated*
*is the small dining room table, the tea cups,*
*two empty chairs, and the microphone.*

*SOUND:*
*Music up.*

*Lights down.*

*End of play.*

(*above*) Tetsuro Shigematsu interviews Mas Yamamoto at 665 Royal Road in North Vancouver, BC. *Bahareh Shigematsu.*

(*below*) Miniature microphone and tea cups created by Susan Miyagishima. *Raymond Shum.*

# East of the Rockies

Though Mas was older when the war ended and we were dispersed east of the Rockies, I was only ten years old. In 1945, when my family left the green valley of Slocan, we found ourselves in the flatlands of the prairies, in the fierce heat and cold and constant wind with the few stumpy trees that grew in Coaldale, Alberta. The harsh environment was one thing. The people were another – kindly Mennonites mostly and other categories of Bible-cherishing Christians.

It's our values, I think, that most define who we are. The capacity to endure grew from sharing in the long days of farm labour that the Japanese Canadian kids had to do. Prudishness and the dread of being cheapened came out of hellfire evangelism. Hatred of the enemy country, Japan, permeated Canadian culture throughout the war and years later. For many, maybe most Nisei, this resulted in the denial of things Japanese. Un-belongingness seeped into our pores. By newspaper headlines and by glances of condescension we grew up as "the only Jap in town."

Possibly the most important value I imbibed was from my mother and my Mennonite friends. Truthfulness mattered. It mattered more than the "group think" in Japanese culture. The Lowen twins who lived three blocks away gasped in shock one night when I said I could tell a fib to my mother in order to stay longer to play. Their shock registered on my inner compass.

Now that I'm eighty-three and living even farther east of the Rockies, mainly in downtown Toronto, I've been engaged in recent days with wondering who we have become. Physically, many grandchildren of the Nisei look Caucasian, Spanish, Latin American, Middle Eastern – hardly Japanese. But apart from the way our mixed-race offspring look, what remains of the values of our ancestors? How have they evolved? What values have endured? What new values have been adopted?

An initiative called We Should Know Each Other has arisen from a curiosity about who we have become but also perhaps from a need for the belongingness that was denied us in our past and that we denied ourselves. Loneliness, of course, is not a Japanese Canadian prerogative. Everywhere humans stretch forth hands, like thirsting roots, seeking water, seeking acceptance and connectedness. In the end, it seems to me, it is not in country, nor ethnicity, nor even in family where we find our truest home, but among those with whom we share our deepest and highest values.

—JOY KOGAWA

## Acknowledgments

TO THE AYUKAWAS. Thank you for allowing me to include your mother's story, and for so generously opening up her photo album to the world.

TO LISA UYEDA. Thank you for pointing me toward our community's equivalent of the Zapruder film. While many photographs of internment exist, what you helped bring into 1 *Hour Photo* is the only known footage to have survived. When you first fed those 8mm loops through the film viewer, I will never forget as we watched those beautiful Nikkei children spring to life, unlocked from the amber of time.

TO LINDA REID AND THE NIKKEI NATIONAL MUSEUM AND CULTURAL CENTRE. From lending us scale models of the tarpaper shacks, to helping me finalize the list of the internment camps, you have always been so generous with your scholarly expertise. If 1 *Hour Photo* ever reached for the stars, it was because you helped root our story in the ground of history.

TO ANN-MARIE METTEN. My journey from the stage to the page has been delightful and illuminating because of your impeccable taste and keen intelligence. Thank you for making me look smarter than I am.

TO MARK AND YUKARI. If my life's work is an ultra-marathon, then your friendship is a cold cup of water placed in my hand. Thank you for refreshing my spirit.

TO HEIDI TAYLOR. Thank you for being my not-so-secret weapon, and for helping me find the connections between the personal and the geopolitical.

**TO RICHARD WOLFE.** Thank you for taking my rough handful of sea glass and creating such sparkling gemstones with your lapidary talents.

**TO STEVEN CHARLES.** Thank you for being so fully present and giving as an artist and as a human being at every stage. I loved standing in the spotlight with you, brother.

**TO GERALD AND PAM.** My impossible task as a writer is to craft lines as elegant as the resplendent worlds you create.

**TO LAURA FUKUMOTO.** Whether it is reading something you write, listening to a story you perform, or wearing the clothing you craft, I am such a fan of your artistry. Thank you for bringing such beauty into my life.

**TO SUSAN MIYAGISHIMA.** Because of your gorgeous handiwork, *1 Hour Photo* won Vancouver Asian Canadian Theatre our first Jessie. You are already a part of our company's past. May you always be a part of our future.

**TO HEATHER REDFERN.** Thank you for taking a chance on me, again and again. My words in your house have made for the most beautiful hauntings. May we conjure many more spirits together.

**TO OLIVIA.** When night falls and dreams will not come, your fiery words warm my hands, and make the shadows dance. Long may they burn.

**TO YOSHIKO SHIGEMATSU.** Second only to Mas himself, you know the entirety of his vast story more than anyone. Thank you for the countless hours you devoted to transcribing. If it weren't for you, *1 Hour Photo* would remain a mass of audiotape. Thank you for painstakingly mining every minute, and for being not just the best grandmother to our children, but an angel in our home.

**TO NAOMI YAMAMOTO.** Nothing I will ever write or perform will be as meaningful as your apology on behalf of the government for interning Japanese Canadians during World War II, from the Fourth Session of the 39th Parliament. Thank you for allowing me to include this historic moment, and for always being such a fierce ally.

TO DONNA YAMAMOTO. Thank you for making so many of my dreams come true, including this one. You are a good daughter. You are a good friend. Your presence in my life is a blessing beyond compare.

TO MAS YAMAMOTO. Thank you for trusting me throughout this journey. Through this play, and now this book, your life will continue to inspire more people than you can ever know. Your friendship has been such a gift to me.

TO BAHAREH. If I were to be handed the dice of fate to change everything in my next life, my gender, my sexuality, my class, my race, I would fling my destiny to the wind, but only if I could hold fast to you. Our love is the only point of stillness for me within this vast and whirling universe.

## Tetsuro Shigematsu

For more than twenty years, Tetsuro Shigematsu has been telling stories across an array of media. He is a writer, actor, performance artist, broadcaster, scholar, filmmaker, and theatre artist. Originally trained in the fine arts, he found a similar creative outlet writing for CBC Television's *This Hour Has 22 Minutes*. In 2004, he became the first person of colour to host a daily national radio program in Canada when he took over *The Roundup* on CBC Radio, where he co-wrote and co-produced nearly a thousand hours of network programming. His earlier theatre work, *Empire of the Son*, sold out its run before it opened and was named the best show of 2015 by the *Vancouver Sun* and the *Georgia Straight* and has toured across Canada and internationally. Tetsuro's award-winning body of work in film, television, radio, new media, and theatre continues to be taught in schools and universities as examples of cultural possibility. *1 Hour Photo* was nominated for five 2018 Jessie Richardson Theatre Awards, including for Outstanding Original Script and Significant Artistic Achievement – Small Theatre for the production's outstanding technical design and execution for the purpose of historical storytelling. His two greatest masterpieces are his children, Mika and Taizo, who inherited their beauty and kindness from their mother, Bahareh. Follow him @tweetsuro or shiggy.com.